This Journal belongs to

____

64507545R00062

Made in the USA
Middletown, DE
14 February 2018